Size Doesn't Matter

Michele Prudlo

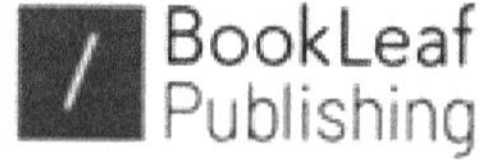

BookLeaf Publishing

Presentation by *BookLeaf Publishing*

Web: www.bookleafpub.com

E-mail: info@bookleafpub.com

ISBN: 9789357211314

First edition 2022

DEDICATION

To my husband who has been there for me through every single project I ever started. He always supports me during happy and difficult times, as well as lets me quit as long as those decisions bring me peace and happiness.

Without you I would have never believed that I would ever meet, especially be with a person that is so generous, forgiving and strong. I am dedicating this book to you because like this book, there are billions of books, and people out there, but you are that special one.

I want to dedicate this book to him because he is that one person that always holds onto me, even when things get so bad that letting go would only make sense.

ACKNOWLEDGEMENT

I would like to acknowledge and thank the universe as well as our father, God. With our physical body, mind and soul, we are able to experience the big, as well as the small things in life.

Every single person I have ever met, spoken to, loved, hated and been in indifference with deserves to be acknowledged because without you, I wouldn't be who I am today.

Last but not least, I want to thank the Bookleaf Publishing team that gives us poets a safe place to pour out our poetry.

PREFACE

I got inspired to write this book after my first two other books were complete. I wanted to challenge myself to see if I can get the most powerful poems out of me with as little words as possible. Less is more. Important words get lost when you squeeze them in with so many meaningless words.

Like humans over explain sometimes, can we come to the point of what we really mean?

My purpose is to make my readers think, realizing that we can all relate to each other in some way. We are not alone.

Remember that the pain doesn't fade, we just get used to living with it.

The Unknown

What if I left the
Known,
For the
Unknown,
Just to be left in:
The Uncomfortable Zone.

With Pain

2

Remember,
It never gets easier,
We just get used to living with the pain.

Karmic Cycled Love

Every single lifetime I make the same mistakes,
Purposely,
Over and over again,
To assure I am brought back to earth,
To meet you again.
You; my love,
Are my karmic cycle.

Soulmates

Let's sign the contract that you'll recognize ,
And love me,
In every single lifetime,
No matter who I show up as.

Twin Flame

5

We ignite the fire in each other;
But we also leave each other behind with burn
marks.

Red String

Our destiny of meeting has been build,
And planned out,
Like a bridge.
There is no U-turn possible,
But this one and only way straight ahead to you.

When You Are Not Here

Water is essential -
Fire is essential -
Air is essential -

But the Earth :
Is not essential -

When -
You are not here;

The Truth

8

The Truth is,
The Truth never wins.

Time Of Death

Isn't it messed up
Knowing,
That everyone else
Will know,
But ourselves,
When we pass away.

Like A Butterfly

I want our love to be symmetrical.
Beautiful and light,
Free and curious
Like a Butterfly.

Tone It Down

When people say:
"Please tone it down"
Do they mean,
Please stop being yourself?

Plastic

You put this ring on me,
I knew it means infinity, forever.
When I fell and rolled down the stairs,
The ring broke in half,
I didn't know at the time,
You gave me a breakable plastic circle.

Truth VS. Lie

We never get rewarded for telling the truth,
But,
We get punished for every single lie.

Clock Out

Now I can clock out,
I can say whatever I want to,
I can do whatever I want to,
I can be whoever I want to.
-Alcohol

Your Soul

I see your soul,
Through your eyes.
Even when you are not here for me to see.

I feel your soul,
By your presence,
Even when you're not here for me to feel.

I know your soul,
Even when you're not introducing yourself.
Because you are the other half of my soul.

The Gate To My Heart

You open the gate to my heart,
Simply,
When you brush my hair out of my face.

Confused Mind

Appreciate the confusion you feel inside of you,
The endless wandering mind,
It means you are still open minded to walk either
path.

You are no longer walking down the one way
road,
Which was rocky and steep,
On the hill you could have easily fallen off of.

Authentic Self

It is the little things that you say,
It is the little things you do,
It is the little bit you have,
To be able to be a lot more of you,
Your authentic self,
That makes your soul shine from the inside out.

Empty

I sit in silence and cry,
I feel so alone without you.
The silence means nothing when you are not
besides me.
The tears mean nothing when you are not wiping
them away.

The cold and salty tears,
Are empty.
The silence,
Feels empty.
The agony,
Purely empty.

Looking Back

Only look back,
When the pain and tears-
have turned into peace.

Dead End

Is it a dead end though?
When I see you there:
Standing,
Waiting,
For ME,
You in a suit,
Roses in your hands,
Your eyes locked with mine,
The keys to unlock- forever lost,
At the dead end.